CONFLICT RESOLUTION ESSENTIALS: A QUICK GUIDE

Navigating Disagreements with Clarity and Compassion.

JAMES C. CLEVER

All books by James C. Clever

- Wonderful Phrases For Solving Conflicts And Managing Difficult People
- Helping A Negative Spouse
- Unlocking Your Hidden Creative Genius
- Overcoming Overthinking And Rumination
- Dealing With Anxiety In A Relationship
- Becoming A Good, Better And Perfect Husband
- Becoming A Good, Better And Perfect Wife
- The Ideal Habits in Relationships
- How To Master Your Emotions And Feelings
- How to Tell or Write a Story Effectively

TABLE OF CONTENTS

INTRODUCTION

In the quiet hum of a bustling office, where the rhythm of productivity often harmonizes with the occasional discord of differing opinions, Sarah found herself at a crossroads. Tensions were rising, and the once cohesive team seemed entangled in a web of misunderstandings. Faced with the challenge of resolving conflicts that threatened the very fabric of collaboration, Sarah embarked on a journey—a journey fueled by the principles you're about to explore in "Conflict Resolution Essentials: A Quick Guide."

This guide isn't just a collection of strategies; it's a compass that points toward harmonious workplaces and flourishing relationships. Picture a scenario where Sarah, armed with the insights within these pages, transformed conflicts into catalysts for team cohesion. The impact rippled through the organization, fostering an environment where individuals felt heard, conflicts were faced head-on, and resolutions were not just solutions but opportunities for growth.

Now, step into the world of conflict resolution, where each page is a key unlocking the potential for positive transformation. As we unravel the essentials, consider the power they hold—the power to turn discord into collaboration, challenges into opportunities, and workplaces into thriving ecosystems of innovation.

Let this quick guide be your companion on a journey where conflicts become stepping stones toward a future where understanding, resolution, and growth intertwine. Welcome to "Conflict Resolution Essentials: A Quick Guide," where the impact is not just read but felt in the very pulse of your professional and personal interactions.

CHAPTER 1

UNDERSTANDING CONFLICT

Conflict is an inherent part of human interaction, and learning how to navigate it is essential for personal and professional growth.

This handbook offers practical insights and actionable strategies to help you comprehend, manage, and ultimately resolve conflicts with clarity and empathy

WHAT IS CONFLICT?

Conflict refers to a disagreement or struggle between two or more parties with opposing interests, needs, or values. It is a natural and inevitable aspect of human interactions, arising from differences in perspectives, goals, or expectations.

Conflicts can occur in various settings, including personal relationships, workplaces, communities, and even at a global scale.

Conflicts can manifest in different forms, ranging from verbal disputes and misunderstandings to more complex and entrenched issues. They may arise due to a variety of reasons, such as:

Miscommunication: Lack of clear communication can lead to misunderstandings and conflicts.

Differing Interests or Goals: When individuals or groups have conflicting objectives or priorities.

Scarce Resources: Competition for limited resources can lead to conflicts over access and allocation.

Values and Beliefs: Differences in personal or cultural values may contribute to conflicts.

Power Imbalances: Unequal distribution of power and influence can lead to conflicts.

Understanding and effectively managing conflicts is crucial for maintaining healthy relationships, fostering cooperation, and promoting positive outcomes.

Conflict resolution involves finding mutually acceptable solutions and addressing underlying issues to achieve a more constructive and harmonious environment.

Successful conflict resolution often requires effective communication, empathy, negotiation, and, in some cases, compromise.

TYPES OF CONFLICT: INTERPERSONAL, ORGANIZATIONAL, AND BEYOND

Conflict is a multifaceted phenomenon, manifesting in various forms and contexts.

Understanding the distinct types of conflict is crucial for developing targeted strategies for resolution.

Here, we explore three primary categories: interpersonal conflict, organizational conflict, and conflicts beyond these immediate settings.

❖ INTERPERSONAL CONFLICT

Interpersonal conflicts occur between individuals and are often rooted in differences in personalities, communication styles, or personal values. Examples include disagreements between friends, family members, or colleagues. Common triggers include misunderstandings, unmet expectations, or differing priorities. Effective resolution typically involves open communication, active listening, and finding common ground.

❖ ORGANIZATIONAL CONFLICT

Organizational conflicts arise within the structures of institutions, businesses, or groups.

These conflicts may involve disagreements between employees, teams, or departments. Common sources include resource allocation, role ambiguity, and conflicting goals.

Addressing organizational conflicts requires a combination of clear communication, strategic leadership, and structured conflict resolution processes to maintain a healthy work environment.

❖ CONFLICTS BEYOND IMMEDIATE SETTINGS

Conflicts can extend beyond interpersonal and organizational boundaries to include broader societal, cultural, or geopolitical issues. These conflicts may involve nations, ethnic groups, or ideologies.

Rooted in historical, political, or economic factors, resolving such conflicts often requires diplomatic efforts, international cooperation, and addressing deep-seated systemic issues.

COMMON THEMES ACROSS TYPES

a. Communication Breakdown:

In all types of conflict, communication plays a central role. Misunderstandings, lack of clarity, or ineffective communication strategies can escalate conflicts.

Active listening and clear expression of ideas are crucial for conflict resolution.

b. Differing Goals and Priorities:

Conflicts often arise from differences in objectives or priorities. Identifying shared goals and finding compromises are essential elements in resolving conflicts across all levels.

c. Power Dynamics:

Power imbalances can contribute to conflicts. Whether in interpersonal relationships, within organizations, or on a global scale, addressing power differentials is vital for achieving fair and sustainable resolutions.

Understanding the nuances of these conflict types enables individuals, leaders, and policymakers to tailor their approaches to effectively manage and resolve conflicts.

By employing a combination of communication skills, empathy, and strategic problem-solving, it becomes possible to transform conflicts into opportunities for growth and positive change.

THE INEVITABILITY OF CONFLICT IN HUMAN INTERACTIONS

Conflict is an inescapable component of human interactions. As individuals with unique perspectives, experiences, and values, clashes of opinions and interests are bound to occur.

Recognizing the inevitability of conflict is the first step toward developing a healthy and constructive approach to managing these challenges.

❖ DIVERSE PERSPECTIVES

Human beings possess diverse backgrounds, cultural influences, and life experiences.

These differences enrich our interactions but also create fertile ground for conflicting viewpoints.

Disagreements can arise due to varied interpretations, beliefs, and ways of approaching situations.

❖ LIMITED RESOURCES

Competition for limited resources—whether tangible like money, time, or space, or intangible like attention and recognition—can breed conflict. Individuals or groups may find themselves at odds when striving to fulfill their needs or secure a share of these resources.

❖ COMMUNICATION CHALLENGES

Communication, despite being a fundamental aspect of human interaction, is fraught with potential for misunderstandings.

Differences in communication styles, preferences, or language can lead to misinterpretations, sparking conflicts even when the underlying intentions are positive.

❖ UNMET EXPECTATIONS

Expectations, whether explicit or implicit, play a significant role in human relationships. When these expectations are not met, disappointment can transform into conflict. Aligning expectations and communicating openly about them can mitigate potential issues.

❖ INDIVIDUAL GOALS AND AMBITIONS

Each person harbors unique aspirations and ambitions. Conflicts may arise when individual goals clash with those of others, leading to competition or discord. Balancing personal objectives with collective needs is a perpetual challenge.

NAVIGATING CONFLICT

Rather than viewing conflict as inherently negative, embracing it as a natural part of human interaction allows for the development of constructive conflict resolution skills.

Proactively addressing conflicts can lead to improved understanding, stronger relationships, and innovative solutions.

STRATEGIES FOR CONSTRUCTIVE CONFLICT RESOLUTION

Open Communication: Encourage transparent and honest dialogue to understand diverse perspectives.

Active Listening: Foster a culture of listening to comprehend the underlying motivations and concerns of others.

Empathy: Cultivate empathy to appreciate the emotions and experiences of those involved in the conflict.

Collaborative Problem-Solving: Shift the focus from winning to finding mutually beneficial solutions.

Negotiation and Compromise: Seek middle ground where conflicting parties can compromise without compromising core values.

Conflict is not an aberration but an integral part of the human experience.

By acknowledging its inevitability and approaching conflicts with a proactive and constructive mindset, individuals and societies can turn these challenges into opportunities for growth, understanding, and positive change.

CHAPTER 2

IDENTIFYING ROOT CAUSES

Conflict resolution begins with a deep understanding of the underlying factors that contribute to discord. Identifying the root causes of conflicts is a pivotal step toward developing targeted and effective strategies for resolution. In this chapter, we delve into the various elements that give rise to conflicts, exploring proactive approaches to address these issues before they escalate.

❖ MISCOMMUNICATION AND LACK OF CLARITY

Root Cause: **Many conflicts stem from** miscommunication, where intentions are misunderstood, messages are unclear, or assumptions lead to confusion.

Resolution Strategy: **Emphasize clear and open** communication. Encourage individuals to express themselves honestly and actively listen to ensure mutual understanding.

❖ UNMET NEEDS AND EXPECTATIONS

Root Cause: **Conflicts often arise when individuals or groups feel their needs are not being met, or expectations are not fulfilled.**

Resolution Strategy: **Facilitate discussions to identify and articulate needs and expectations. Encourage negotiation and compromise to find common ground.**

❖ DIFFERING VALUES AND PERSPECTIVES

Root Cause: **Conflicts may arise due to fundamental differences in values, beliefs, or cultural perspectives.**

Resolution Strategy: **Foster cultural competence and empathy. Create spaces for open dialogue to enhance understanding and appreciation for diverse viewpoints.**

❖ SCARCE RESOURCES

Root Cause: **Competition for limited resources, whether tangible (e.g., budget, time) or intangible (e.g., recognition, opportunities), can lead to conflicts.**

Resolution Strategy: **Implement fair resource allocation systems. Encourage collaboration to optimize resource use and minimize competition.**

❖ ROLE AMBIGUITY AND RESPONSIBILITIES

Root Cause: **Lack of clarity regarding roles and responsibilities** within a group or organization can lead to confusion and conflict.

Resolution Strategy: **Clearly define roles and responsibilities.** Establish effective communication channels to address concerns and provide feedback.

❖ PERSONALITY CLASHES

Root Cause: **Conflicts may arise from differences in** personality traits, communication styles, or working preferences.

Resolution Strategy: **Promote team-building activities to** enhance understanding and appreciation of diverse personalities. Encourage open communication to address potential clashes.

❖ UNRESOLVED PAST ISSUES

Root Cause: **Lingering resentments or unresolved past** conflicts can contribute to current discord.

Resolution Strategy: **Address historical issues proactively.** Facilitate discussions to acknowledge past grievances and work towards reconciliation.

❖ EXTERNAL INFLUENCES

Root Cause: **Conflicts can be influenced by external factors such as societal trends, economic pressures, or political unrest.**

Resolution Strategy: **Stay informed about external influences.** Adapt communication and strategies to navigate and minimize the impact of external pressures.

Identifying the root causes of conflicts is a crucial step in the journey towards resolution. By acknowledging and addressing these underlying issues, individuals and groups can lay the foundation for more effective conflict management. The next chapters will explore strategies for proactive conflict resolution based on a comprehensive understanding of these root causes.

CHAPTER 3

PROACTIVE CONFLICT MANAGEMENT:

ADDRESSING ISSUES BEFORE THEY ESCALATE

Proactive conflict management is the art of anticipating and addressing potential issues before they escalate into more significant challenges.

By identifying early warning signs and implementing strategies to promote open communication and understanding, individuals and organizations can create a culture that prevents conflicts from reaching a critical stage.

In this chapter, we explore the principles and practices of proactive conflict management.

❖ EARLY DETECTION AND WARNING SIGNS

Identification: Train individuals to recognize early signs of tension or dissatisfaction, such as increased stress, decreased communication, or subtle changes in behavior.

Intervention: Establish mechanisms for reporting and addressing concerns promptly. Encourage open communication channels for individuals to express their grievances or discomfort.

❖ CLEAR COMMUNICATION CHANNELS:

Proactive Communication: Foster an environment where individuals feel comfortable expressing their thoughts and concerns without fear of reprisal.

Conflict Resolution Platforms: Implement accessible platforms, such as suggestion boxes or anonymous reporting systems, to encourage individuals to share potential issues.

❖ REGULAR CHECK-INS AND FEEDBACK

Scheduled Assessments: Conduct regular check-ins or evaluations to assess team dynamics and individual satisfaction.

Feedback Mechanisms: Establish feedback loops to gather insights on potential sources of conflict, allowing for timely intervention and resolution.

❖ CONFLICT Resolution Training

Education and Training: **Provide** training sessions on conflict resolution skills, emphasizing the importance of proactive approaches to prevent conflicts.

Empowerment: **Equip** individuals with the tools to address conflicts at an early stage, promoting a sense of empowerment and responsibility.

❖ TEAM-BUILDING ACTIVITIES

Promoting Cohesion: **Organize** team-building activities to enhance interpersonal relationships and foster a positive team culture.

Building Trust: **Strengthening** trust within a group can act as a preventive measure, reducing the likelihood of conflicts arising.

❖ LEADERSHIP INVOLVEMENT

Visible Leadership: **Encourage** leaders to be actively involved in conflict prevention efforts, setting an example for the rest of the team.

Conflict Resolution Training for Leaders: **Equip leaders** with the skills to identify potential conflicts and address them proactively.

❖ DIVERSITY AND INCLUSION INITIATIVES

Promoting Understanding: **Embrace diversity and** inclusion initiatives to minimize potential sources of conflict related to differing backgrounds, perspectives, or experiences.

Cultural Competence: **Foster a culture of cultural** competence, where individuals appreciate and learn from diverse viewpoints.

❖ ESTABLISHING A CONFLICT
   RESOLUTION FRAMEWORK:

Written Policies: **Develop clear and accessible conflict** resolution policies within organizations.

Structured Processes: **Define step-by-step processes for** addressing conflicts, ensuring a systematic and fair approach.

Proactive conflict management is an investment in the health and sustainability of relationships, both in personal and professional settings.

By cultivating a culture that addresses issues before they escalate, individuals and organizations can foster a harmonious environment where conflicts are opportunities for growth and understanding, rather than obstacles to success.

The next chapters will delve into specific strategies and techniques for resolving conflicts proactively.

CHAPTER 4

PROACTIVE CONFLICT RESOLUTION

STRATEGIES AND TECHNIQUES

Proactively resolving conflicts requires a strategic and systematic approach that goes beyond mere identification.

In this chapter, we explore specific strategies and techniques designed to address conflicts at their roots, fostering understanding and collaboration before tensions escalate.

❖ CONSTRUCTIVE COMMUNICATION WORKSHOPS

Interactive Sessions: Conduct workshops focused on effective communication strategies, emphasizing active listening, clear expression, and nonviolent communication techniques.

Team-Based Learning: Encourage team participation to promote a shared understanding of communication dynamics, reducing the potential for misinterpretation and conflict.

❖ CONFLICT MAPPING AND ANALYSIS

Identification of Patterns: **Train individuals or teams to map past conflicts, identifying recurring patterns or triggers.**

Root Cause Analysis: **Conduct in-depth analyses to identify the underlying issues contributing to conflicts, allowing for targeted prevention efforts.**

❖ EMOTIONAL INTELLIGENCE TRAINING

Emotional Awareness: **Provide training on emotional intelligence to enhance individuals' awareness and management of their own emotions and those of others.**

Empathy Building: **Cultivate empathy as a tool for understanding diverse perspectives and reducing emotional tension.**

❖ MEDIATION SKILLS DEVELOPMENT

Neutral Facilitation: **Train designated individuals or leaders in mediation skills to facilitate constructive dialogues between conflicting parties.**

Conflict Resolution Simulation: **Conduct simulations to hone mediation skills in realistic scenarios, preparing individuals for proactive conflict resolution.**

❖ PEER SUPPORT PROGRAMS

Buddy Systems: **Establish peer support programs where individuals have designated allies to whom they can turn for advice or assistance.**

Mediation Pairs: **Pair individuals with complementary conflict resolution skills to provide mutual support within teams.**

❖ ROLE-PLAYING EXERCISES

Scenario-Based Training: **Conduct role-playing exercises simulating potential conflict situations.**

Solution-Focused Practice: **Encourage participants to explore and practice solutions in a controlled environment, enhancing their conflict resolution skills.**

❖ TEAM-BUILDING RETREATS

Structured Retreats: **Organize team-building retreats with structured activities designed to strengthen team cohesion.**

Open Discussions: **Create spaces for open discussions about potential conflicts and strategies for preventing them in the future.**

❖ TRANSPARENT DECISION-MAKING PROCESSES

Inclusive Decision-Making: **Ensure that decision-making processes are transparent and inclusive, reducing feelings of exclusion that can lead to conflicts.**

Feedback Mechanisms: **Establish feedback loops to address concerns about decision-making processes proactively.**

❖ CONTINUOUS FEEDBACK LOOPS

Regular Check-ins: **Implement ongoing check-ins to assess team dynamics, satisfaction, and potential sources of tension.**

Anonymous Feedback Systems: **Allow** individuals to provide feedback anonymously, encouraging open and honest communication.

Proactive conflict resolution is an ongoing process that requires a commitment to continuous improvement and learning.

By implementing these specific strategies and techniques, individuals and organizations can create a culture that not only addresses conflicts as they arise but actively works to prevent them, fostering a positive and collaborative environment.

The subsequent chapters will explore real-world applications and case studies of these proactive conflict resolution strategies in action.

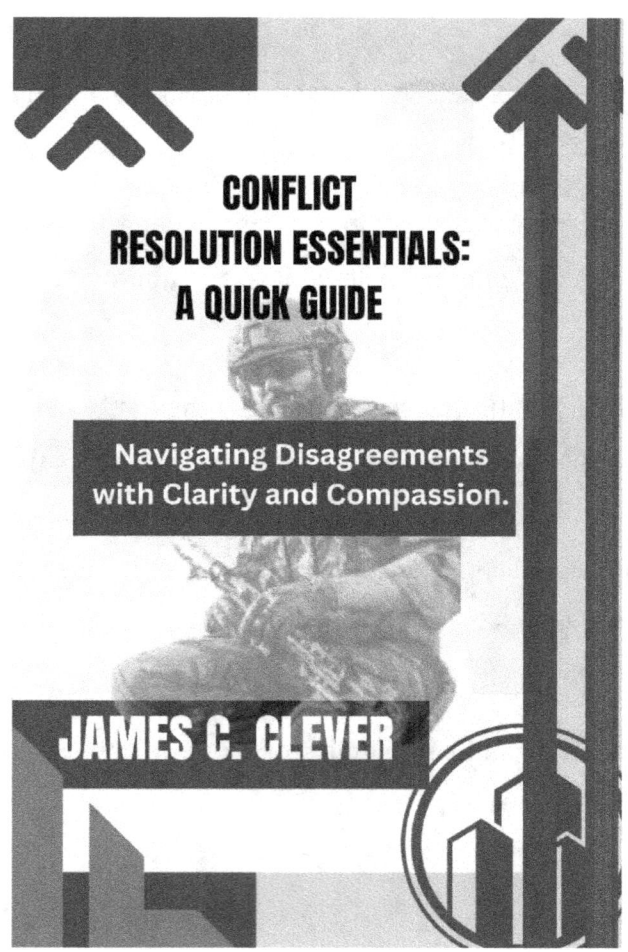

CHAPTER 5

REAL-WORLD APPLICATIONS AND CASE STUDIES

In this chapter, we explore real-world applications of proactive conflict resolution strategies and delve into case studies that showcase the successful implementation of these techniques in various settings.

- ❖ COMMUNICATION WORKSHOPS IN A CORPORATE SETTING:

Context: A multinational corporation identified frequent misunderstandings and conflicts among team members, leading to decreased productivity.

Strategy: Implemented constructive communication workshops focusing on active listening, effective expression, and nonviolent communication.

Results: Enhanced communication skills led to better understanding, improved collaboration, and a noticeable reduction in conflicts. Teams reported increased satisfaction and productivity.

❖ CONFLICT MAPPING IN A NONPROFIT ORGANIZATION

Context: A nonprofit organization observed recurring conflicts among volunteers and staff members, hindering the achievement of organizational goals.

Strategy: Conducted conflict mapping and analysis to identify patterns and root causes of conflicts. Based on the data, we implemented specific strategies.

Results: By addressing the root causes, the organization experienced improved volunteer morale, increased cooperation, and a more positive organizational culture.

❖ EMOTIONAL INTELLIGENCE TRAINING IN HEALTHCARE

Context: A healthcare institution noticed tension among staff members, affecting the overall work environment and patient care.

Strategy: Introduced emotional intelligence training to enhance self-awareness and empathy among healthcare professionals.

Results: Staff members reported a better understanding of their own emotions and those of their colleagues. The improved emotional intelligence contributed to a more supportive work environment and enhanced patient care.

❖ PEER SUPPORT PROGRAM IN EDUCATIONAL INSTITUTIONS

Context: A university observed conflicts among students, particularly during group projects and collaborative activities.

Strategy: Implemented a peer support program where students were paired with designated allies for advice and assistance. Included mediation pairs for conflict resolution.

Results: The peer support program created a sense of community among students, reduced conflicts, and provided a support system for individuals facing academic or personal challenges.

❖ ROLE-PLAYING EXERCISES IN A
    GOVERNMENT AGENCY

Context: A government agency faced challenges in interdepartmental communication, leading to misunderstandings and delays in project completion.

Strategy: Conducted role-playing exercises simulating potential conflict scenarios and solution-focused practices during team-building sessions.

Results: Improved communication and problem-solving skills led to smoother interdepartmental collaboration, reducing conflicts and enhancing overall efficiency in project delivery.

❖ TRANSPARENT DECISION-MAKING IN A
    NON-GOVERNMENTAL ORGANIZATION
    (NGO)

Context: An NGO encountered conflicts arising from perceived inequities in decision-making processes.

Strategy: Implemented transparent decision-making processes, ensuring inclusivity and establishing feedback mechanisms for continuous improvement.

Results: Increased transparency led to greater trust among team members, reduced conflicts related to decision-making, and a more harmonious working environment.

❖ CONTINUOUS FEEDBACK LOOPS IN TECHNOLOGY STARTUPS

Context: A tech startup faced challenges in retaining talent due to conflicts and dissatisfaction among team members.

Strategy: Introduced regular check-ins and anonymous feedback systems to address concerns proactively and improve team dynamics.

Results: Increased job satisfaction, lower turnover rates, and a more adaptive and collaborative work culture were observed, contributing to the startup's success.

These case studies highlight the adaptability and effectiveness of proactive conflict resolution strategies across diverse contexts. By tailoring these strategies to specific organizational needs and fostering a culture of continuous improvement, individuals and organizations can create environments where conflicts are not just managed but prevented, leading to sustained success and positive outcomes. The final chapters will provide practical tips for integrating these strategies into various organizational structures and offer guidance on maintaining a proactive conflict resolution approach over time.

CHAPTER 6

PRACTICAL TIPS FOR INTEGRATION AND MAINTENANCE OF PROACTIVE CONFLICT RESOLUTION STRATEGIES

Effectively integrating proactive conflict resolution strategies into various organizational structures requires a thoughtful and sustained effort. In this chapter, we provide practical tips for seamlessly incorporating these strategies and offer guidance on maintaining a proactive conflict resolution approach over time.

CUSTOMIZE STRATEGIES TO ORGANIZATIONAL CULTURE

Tip: Tailor conflict resolution strategies to align with the existing culture, values, and structure of the organization.

Guidance: Understand the unique dynamics of the organization, ensuring that conflict resolution strategies resonate with employees and leadership. This enhances the likelihood of successful integration and long-term sustainability.

❖ LEADERSHIP ENDORSEMENT AND PARTICIPATION

Tip: Ensure active involvement and endorsement from leadership throughout the implementation process.

Guidance: Leaders should model proactive conflict resolution behaviors, participate in training, and consistently communicate the importance of these strategies to the organization. This reinforces a culture of conflict resolution at all levels.

❖ CONTINUOUS TRAINING AND SKILL DEVELOPMENT

Tip: Implement ongoing training programs to continually develop conflict resolution skills among employees.

Guidance: Regular workshops, seminars, and skill-building sessions help reinforce conflict resolution techniques. This approach ensures that employees remain adept at identifying and addressing conflicts proactively.

❖ INTEGRATION INTO PERFORMANCE EVALUATIONS

Tip: Integrate conflict resolution competencies into performance evaluations and feedback mechanisms.

Guidance: By incorporating conflict resolution skills as a part of performance assessments, employees are motivated to prioritize these skills, fostering a culture where conflict resolution becomes an integral aspect of professional development.

❖ ESTABLISH CLEAR POLICIES AND PROCEDURES

Tip: Develop and communicate clear conflict resolution policies and procedures within the organization.

Guidance: Clearly defined processes for reporting and addressing conflicts provide a structured framework. This transparency empowers individuals to navigate conflicts confidently and contributes to a culture of openness.

❖ FOSTER A COLLABORATIVE ENVIRONMENT

Tip: Encourage collaborative environments that emphasize teamwork and shared goals.

Guidance: By fostering a collaborative mindset, individuals are more likely to proactively address conflicts, viewing them as opportunities for collective growth rather than as obstacles.

❖ FEEDBACK MECHANISMS FOR IMPROVEMENT

Tip: Establish continuous feedback loops to gather insights on the effectiveness of conflict resolution strategies.

Guidance: Regularly solicit feedback from employees to identify areas for improvement and adaptation. This ensures that conflict resolution strategies remain relevant and responsive to the evolving needs of the organization.

❖ INCENTIVIZE PROACTIVE CONFLICT RESOLUTION

Tip: Recognize and reward instances of effective proactive conflict resolution.

Guidance: Incentives, whether tangible or intangible, motivate employees to actively engage in conflict resolution efforts. Recognition programs can highlight individuals or teams that exemplify proactive conflict resolution.

❖ REGULARLY ASSESS ORGANIZATIONAL CLIMATE

Tip: Conduct periodic assessments of the organizational climate regarding conflict resolution.

Guidance: Regularly evaluate the effectiveness of conflict resolution strategies and their impact on the overall organizational climate. Adjust strategies as needed to address emerging challenges and maintain relevance.

❖ CULTIVATE A LEARNING CULTURE

Tip: Promote a culture of continuous learning, where mistakes are viewed as opportunities for improvement.

Guidance: Encourage a mindset that values learning from conflicts and sees them as integral to growth. This approach fosters resilience and adaptability within the organization.

Integrating and maintaining proactive conflict resolution strategies in organizational structures is an ongoing process that requires commitment, adaptability, and continuous improvement. By following these practical tips and providing consistent guidance, organizations can cultivate an environment where conflicts are approached proactively, contributing to a healthier and more productive workplace. The final chapter will provide a comprehensive summary and offer insights into the future of proactive conflict resolution in evolving organizational landscapes.

CHAPTER 7

COMPREHENSIVE SUMMARY AND FUTURE INSIGHTS

In this final chapter, we present a comprehensive summary of the key concepts discussed throughout the book and offer insights into the future of proactive conflict resolution in evolving organizational landscapes.

COMPREHENSIVE SUMMARY

Understanding Conflict:

- ✓ Conflict is inevitable in human interactions, arising from diverse perspectives, needs, and values.
- ✓ Key causes include miscommunication, unmet needs, differing values, and power imbalances.

Identifying Root Causes:

- ✓ Proactive conflict resolution begins with recognizing and addressing the underlying factors contributing to conflicts.
- ✓ Root causes can range from communication breakdowns to unresolved past issues.

Proactive Conflict Management: **Addressing Issues Before They Escalate**

- ✓ Early detection and warning signs are crucial for intervention before conflicts escalate.
- ✓ Strategies include clear communication channels, regular check-ins, and conflict resolution training.

Proactive Conflict Resolution Strategies and Techniques:

- ✓ Constructive communication workshops enhance essential skills like active listening and nonviolent communication.
- ✓ Conflict mapping, emotional intelligence training, and mediation skills development offer targeted approaches.
- ✓ Peer support programs, role-playing exercises, and transparent decision-making contribute to proactive resolution.
- ✓ Continuous feedback loops and team-building activities foster ongoing conflict resolution efforts.

Real-World Applications and Case Studies:

Case studies illustrate successful applications of proactive conflict resolution strategies in diverse contexts.

Strategies like communication workshops, conflict mapping, emotional intelligence training, and peer support have real-world impact.

Practical Tips for Integration and Maintenance:

- ✓ Customizing strategies to organizational culture enhances alignment and effectiveness.
- ✓ Leadership endorsement, continuous training, and performance evaluations contribute to sustained efforts.
- ✓ Establishing clear policies, fostering collaboration, and incentivizing proactive resolution are vital components.

Insights into the Future of Proactive Conflict Resolution:

a. Technology Integration:

- ✓ Leveraging technology for conflict resolution tools and platforms.

✓ Virtual reality simulations and artificial intelligence to enhance conflict resolution training.

b. Data-Driven Approaches:

✓ Using data analytics to identify patterns and predict potential conflicts.
✓ Incorporating insights from organizational data to tailor conflict resolution strategies.

c. Remote Work Challenges:

✓ Adapting conflict resolution strategies to the challenges posed by remote work.
✓ Emphasizing digital communication skills and virtual team-building activities.

d. Diversity, Equity, and Inclusion (DEI) Initiatives:

✓ Integrating DEI principles into conflict resolution strategies.
✓ Recognizing and addressing conflicts related to diversity and inclusion proactively.

e. Cross-Cultural Competence:

- ✓ Emphasizing cross-cultural competence in conflict resolution training.
- ✓ Preparing individuals and organizations for the challenges of a globalized workforce.

f. Sustainable and Ethical Practices:

- ✓ Incorporating sustainability and ethical considerations into conflict resolution approaches.
- ✓ Addressing conflicts related to environmental concerns and ethical decision-making.

The future of proactive conflict resolution in evolving organizational landscapes is marked by innovation, adaptability, and a commitment to ongoing improvement.

Organizations that embrace technology, data-driven approaches, and a focus on remote work challenges will be better equipped to navigate conflicts proactively.

Additionally, the integration of diversity, equity, and inclusion initiatives, cross-cultural competence, and a commitment to sustainable and ethical practices will contribute to a holistic and resilient approach to conflict resolution.

As organizational landscapes continue to evolve, proactive conflict resolution remains a cornerstone for fostering positive workplace cultures, enhancing collaboration, and achieving sustainable success.

By staying attuned to emerging trends and embracing a proactive mindset, organizations can navigate conflicts effectively and create environments conducive to growth, innovation, and harmonious collaboration.

CONCLUSION

In this concise yet comprehensive guide, we've journeyed through the fundamentals of conflict resolution. From recognizing the inherent nature of conflicts to delving into proactive strategies, this quick guide equips you with essential tools.

As you apply these insights, remember the power of customization—tailoring strategies to your organizational culture and individual dynamics. Embedding conflict resolution into daily practices ensures a culture of collaboration and growth.

Looking ahead, the evolving landscape demands adaptability. Embrace technology, data-driven insights, and inclusivity to future-proof your conflict resolution approach.

May this guide be your quick reference, empowering you to navigate conflicts with confidence, turning them into stepping stones for success and harmonious relationships.

In your ongoing journey, cultivate a mindset that sees conflicts not as roadblocks but as opportunities for improvement. Embrace the continuous learning ethos, where each resolution becomes a lesson and a step toward organizational resilience.

As you integrate these conflict resolution essentials, consider the ripple effect they can have. Your proactive approach not only resolves immediate issues but also sets the tone for a positive work environment, fostering collaboration and innovation.

In a world where change is constant, your commitment to conflict resolution essentials positions you as a leader capable of steering through challenges. Stay agile, keep refining your strategies, and remain open to emerging trends.

Conflict resolution is not just a skill; it's a cornerstone for successful and sustainable organizational dynamics. Here's to a future where conflicts are met with confidence, creativity, and a commitment to building stronger, more resilient teams. May this quick guide continue to serve as a valuable resource in your ongoing pursuit of effective conflict resolution.

www.ingramcontent.com/pod-product-compliance
Lightning Source LLC
Chambersburg PA
CBHW071216290526
45796CB00008B/264